PEACE TWEETS

140 Bits of Intention and Inspiration for Peace
All in 140 Characters or Less

CONTRIBUTING AUTHORS

Bobbi Benson | Joseph Bernard
Bud Bilanich | Mary A. Casey II | Chris Guillebeau | Ani Bell

Peace Together, LLC
Boulder, Colorado | www.peace-together.com
www.peacetogetherjournal.com | www.facebook.com/peacetogether

ACKNOWLEDGEMENT

To peacemakers everywhere.
Think peace, be peace, and act in peace
every moment of every day.

INTRODUCTION

This is a book about awakening your mind to ideas and inspiration about peace — all in 140 characters or less. It's a quick read, but filled with introspections that will make you think — and possibly spark your own journey into action.

Each tweet comes from the heart and experience of the author listening to their inner voice and a strong desire to find their own truth. Ultimately, this is what will lead to world peace. It starts with ourselves. There are plenty of limited thinkers who will try to convince you that peace is impossible. Ignore them. Peace is possible if we want it. Think peace, feel peace and be peace. Aspire to live in peace moment-by-moment.

We hope this book of tweets will help you along your journey, and give you thoughts to ponder, as well as information to share with others.

The first 104 tweets were written by myself and Joseph (my partner in Peace Together and life). He has amazing insight into the potential that we all have, having been a student, teacher, athlete, counselor, coach, artist, author, speaker and social activists for a long time. I learn from him daily. I am blessed with such a wonderful partnership both in life and business. He has a blog and writes a post everyday that will expand your awareness and inspire your life *(www.ExploreLifeBlog.com)*.

The next section, Peace Heroes Tweets, are contributions from our friends and fellow peacemakers. Their insights and tweets are nuggets of brilliant wisdom.

Enjoy the book, and let us know what your thoughts (and tweets) are about peace: *peacetweets@peace-together.com*.

THANK YOU

I am so thankful for the contributors that share my passion for peace and chose to be a part of this project.

The original idea for this came from **Bud Bilanich**, a friend, client and fellow visionary. I designed and produced his book: *Success Tweets (www.SuccessTweets.com)*, and he suggested I do *Peace Tweets*. This book is the result of that discussion. Thanks, Bud!

Mary Casey is my sensei. Everyday I appreciate what she teaches me as I pursue my practice of To-Shin Do. Through that practice I've learned that replacing fear with empowerment makes me a stronger ally for peace and compassion.

I discovered **Chris Guillebeau** through my wanderings on the internet, and instantly loved what he was saying: set your own rules, live the life you want, and change the world. He is doing just that. I love reading about his adventures as he travels the world.

And **Ani Bell** . . . whom I met several years ago and instantly liked. She is a kindred spirit, and now is a "kick-ass" coach that is teaching people how to be a risk-taker, rain-maker and rule-breaker. She has incredible email blasts that she periodically sends out that I can't wait to receive.

To each of you, thank you! I am so grateful for your friendship, your support, and the uniqueness of each of your tweets.

Bobbi Benson
Strategic Creativity Director and Partner, Peace Together

ABOUT PEACE TOGETHER

Peace Together began out of passion and action. When Joseph and I met, one of our common interest was peace and helping each person find peace in their lives. We spent time talking about what was going on in our country and the decisions being made. Instead of complaining we felt like we needed to do something positive. So the seeds of Peace Together began.

Our approach was to create a for-profit business that supports social-profit initiatives through awakening **consciousness,** spreading **compassion** and realizing our **connections** to each other — the 3 Cs.

To support our mission we have designed a line of t-shirts with positive messages of peace. They are produced on 100% organic, pesticide-free cotton (or bamboo), and are printed in an earth-friendly way using the cleanest printing techniques. Our shirts are also sweat-shop free. As our business prospers, we donate to organizations and individuals that are working for peace, and fall within our 3 Cs criteria.

We also partner with other businesses that have like-minded values, and offer their products. We choose products that are unique, crafted with care, and express peace in a special way.

We have a big mission and vision, and will continue to grow Peace Together so that we may help other organizations in their mission.

www.peace-together.com
www.peacetogetherjournal.com
www.facebook.com/peacetogether

We are a small company with a big mission.

TABLE OF CONTENTS

Peace Tweets

Bobbi Benson 9

Joseph Bernard 63

Peace Heroes Tweets 113

Bud Bilanich 114

Mary A. Casey, II 124

Chris Guillebeau 134

Ani Bell 144

1

Finding peace is an inside job. Spend some quiet time away from the clutter of life just being in the moment.

Bobbi Benson | Peace Together
bbenson@Peace-Together.com | www.Peace-Together.com

2

What if someone declared a war, and no one showed up. Fight for peace.

Bobbi Benson | *Peace Together*
bbenson@Peace-Together.com | *www.Peace-Together.com*

3

Connect to each other.
Connect to peace.

Bobbi Benson | Peace Together
bbenson@Peace-Together.com | www.Peace-Together.com

4

Speak peace wherever you go.

Bobbi Benson | *Peace Together*
bbenson@Peace-Together.com | *www.Peace-Together.com*

5

Engage in a dialogue that accepts diversity,
welcomes differences, and connects hearts.

Bobbi Benson | *Peace Together*
bbenson@Peace-Together.com | *www.Peace-Together.com*

6

Ask yourself, what can I do today to contribute to a peaceful world?

Bobbi Benson | *Peace Together*
bbenson@Peace-Together.com | *www.Peace-Together.com*

7

Peace begins with you. Open your heart to love, and you will find peace.

Bobbi Benson | *Peace Together*
bbenson@Peace-Together.com | *www.Peace-Together.com*

8

In between the silence peace will appear.

Bobbi Benson | *Peace Together*
bbenson@Peace-Together.com | *www.Peace-Together.com*

9

Be of service to each other. This will open your heart and create room for inner peace.

Bobbi Benson | Peace Together
bbenson@Peace-Together.com | www.Peace-Together.com

10

Put down your baggage, heal your soul,
and open up to peace and joy.

Bobbi Benson | Peace Together
bbenson@Peace-Together.com | www.Peace-Together.com

11

Do something just for the pure joy of doing it.

Bobbi Benson | Peace Together
bbenson@Peace-Together.com | www.Peace-Together.com

12

Do something nice for someone today.
Totally unexpected and unplanned.

Bobbi Benson | Peace Together
bbenson@Peace-Together.com | www.Peace-Together.com

13

Moment by moment be grateful and
find the blessings in your life.

Bobbi Benson | *Peace Together*
bbenson@Peace-Together.com | *www.Peace-Together.com*

14

Find a state of mind that helps courage to grow and to do what is right and just.

Bobbi Benson | Peace Together
bbenson@Peace-Together.com | www.Peace-Together.com

15

Spend time connected to nature to find inspiration, beauty and peace of mind.

Bobbi Benson | Peace Together
bbenson@Peace-Together.com | www.Peace-Together.com

16

With the joy of freedom comes the
responsibility to keep working
for the freedom of all.

Bobbi Benson | *Peace Together*
bbenson@Peace-Together.com | *www.Peace-Together.com*

17

Help to develop a shared vision of the world
that includes justice, peace and harmony.

Bobbi Benson | *Peace Together*
bbenson@Peace-Together.com | *www.Peace-Together.com*

18

Be bold, be courageous as you dream what
the world can be. Dream a big dream,
then begin to live that dream.

Bobbi Benson | Peace Together
bbenson@Peace-Together.com | www.Peace-Together.com

19

Learn to live on this planet so that all species are considered and our natural environment is treated with respect. Love mother earth.

Bobbi Benson | *Peace Together*
bbenson@Peace-Together.com | *www.Peace-Together.com*

20

Work towards a nuclear-free world. Our future depends on each of us saying "no more weapons, not more war."

Bobbi Benson | Peace Together
bbenson@Peace-Together.com | www.Peace-Together.com

21

Make a commitment to stand for justice, human dignity and freedom for all. When we do that surely peace will come.

Bobbi Benson | Peace Together
bbenson@Peace-Together.com | www.Peace-Together.com

22

Peace begins with a smile. When you greet
someone smile to the one that will do
great things in the world.

Bobbi Benson | Peace Together
bbenson@Peace-Together.com | www.Peace-Together.com

23

Each generation has inspiring people that move our world in some way. Protect the children that will become those inspirations.

Bobbi Benson | Peace Together
bbenson@Peace-Together.com | www.Peace-Together.com

24

Giving in to your anger is easy. Forgiveness
takes courage. Love takes openness.
Peace takes forgiveness and love.

Bobbi Benson | Peace Together
bbenson@Peace-Together.com | www.Peace-Together.com

25

Create joy in your life by being
grateful for all you have.

Bobbi Benson | Peace Together
bbenson@Peace-Together.com | www.Peace-Together.com

26

Finding compassion in our life will lead to peace. Open your heart to an understanding that we are all connected.

Bobbi Benson | Peace Together
bbenson@Peace-Together.com | www.Peace-Together.com

27

Unless we change individually, nothing will change collectively. We can't wait for a more convenient time. We must start now.

Bobbi Benson | Peace Together
bbenson@Peace-Together.com | www.Peace-Together.com

28

To truly create peace in this world, each one of use must cultivate our own peace. And then help it to grow, spread and nourish others.

Bobbi Benson | *Peace Together*
bbenson@Peace-Together.com | *www.Peace-Together.com*

29

Open your hand and let your peace and love
out into the world. Dare to let it fly.

Bobbi Benson | Peace Together
bbenson@Peace-Together.com | www.Peace-Together.com

30

Love and peace are two possessions that you
want to give away freely everyday in every way.

Bobbi Benson | Peace Together
bbenson@Peace-Together.com | www.Peace-Together.com

31

Be the change you want to see in the world.
Really truly be that change. Have the
courage to live it.

Bobbi Benson | *Peace Together*
bbenson@Peace-Together.com | *www.Peace-Together.com*

32

Have a heart of love and peace.

Bobbi Benson | *Peace Together*
bbenson@Peace-Together.com | *www.Peace-Together.com*

33

Practice compassion every time you have
an opportunity to make a choice
about your response.

Bobbi Benson | Peace Together
bbenson@Peace-Together.com | www.Peace-Together.com

34

Recognize our need for harmony. Practice
cooperation and compromise.

Bobbi Benson | *Peace Together*
bbenson@Peace-Together.com | *www.Peace-Together.com*

35

Only a genuine feeling of empathy
for others can really motivate us
to act on their behalf.

Bobbi Benson | *Peace Together*
bbenson@Peace-Together.com | *www.Peace-Together.com*

36

Laughing is good for the soul. Laugh often
and laugh loud. Let that energy spread
to everyone around you.

Bobbi Benson | Peace Together
bbenson@Peace-Together.com | www.Peace-Together.com

37

Create an intention every day that you will
live in peace, spread your joy and
create happiness in all you do.

Bobbi Benson | *Peace Together*
bbenson@Peace-Together.com | *www.Peace-Together.com*

38

Be awake to the present moment, and
live in each moment. Just be.

Bobbi Benson | *Peace Together*
bbenson@Peace-Together.com | *www.Peace-Together.com*

39

Find your peace in being quiet, being present,
being aware of the moment. Bless the now,
and then move to the next.

Bobbi Benson | Peace Together
bbenson@Peace-Together.com | www.Peace-Together.com

40

We are just a moment in time. But we contribute to the whole energy. Choose to contribute peace and love.

Bobbi Benson | Peace Together
bbenson@Peace-Together.com | www.Peace-Together.com

41

If you want to change the world, it has to be person by person. If everyone felt peace, then we would have peace.

Bobbi Benson | Peace Together
bbenson@Peace-Together.com | www.Peace-Together.com

42

Never give into hopelessness. People have
achieved amazing goals against all odds
because they persevered.

Bobbi Benson | Peace Together
bbenson@Peace-Together.com | www.Peace-Together.com

43

Don't give in. Don't give up. Don't' stop.
Just go on. Peace will prevail.

Bobbi Benson | *Peace Together*
bbenson@Peace-Together.com | *www.Peace-Together.com*

44

Respect and the pursuit of the common
good for all humanity will
lead to lasting peace.

Bobbi Benson | Peace Together
bbenson@Peace-Together.com | www.Peace-Together.com

45

Creative expression; music, poetry, visual arts, or dance can change people, and bring us together. We discover our connections.

Bobbi Benson | Peace Together
bbenson@Peace-Together.com | www.Peace-Together.com

46

We cannot rely on others to make peace
happen. We each have to take responsibility
in our own lives to find our peace.

Bobbi Benson | Peace Together
bbenson@Peace-Together.com | www.Peace-Together.com

47

Creating peace is about finding commonality;
it's about compromise and consensus.
It's about seeing the world without conflict.

Bobbi Benson | Peace Together
bbenson@Peace-Together.com | www.Peace-Together.com

48

Get involved in something you are passionate
about. Create a new vision of the
world you want to see.

Bobbi Benson | Peace Together
bbenson@Peace-Together.com | www.Peace-Together.com

49

Consider future generations when you stand up against broken systems that go astray. They are your inspiration to keep moving forward.

Bobbi Benson | *Peace Together*
bbenson@Peace-Together.com | *www.Peace-Together.com*

50

May we all come together in peace. Work for it daily, weekly, monthly and yearly.

Bobbi Benson | Peace Together
bbenson@Peace-Together.com | www.Peace-Together.com

51

Let's declare peace upon the world!

Bobbi Benson | Peace Together
bbenson@Peace-Together.com | www.Peace-Together.com

52

If we all believed in peace, we would have it!

Bobbi Benson | *Peace Together*
bbenson@Peace-Together.com | *www.Peace-Together.com*

53

Find others that want peace in this world as much as you, and work together. Each person you touch with goodness touches others.

Bobbi Benson | *Peace Together*
bbenson@Peace-Together.com | *www.Peace-Together.com*

54

Don't be silent about love and peace.
Live it, feel it, be it everyday.

Bobbi Benson | Peace Together
bbenson@Peace-Together.com | www.Peace-Together.com

55

If you want peace, choose to think
peaceful thoughts.

Joseph Bernard | Peace Together | Explore Life
josephteach@hotmail.com | www.Peace-Together.com | www.ExploreLifeBlog.com

56

Let your mind wonder what will bring peace
to the world. Your mind will have many
ideas but your heart is a better guide.

Joseph Bernard | Peace Together | Explore Life
josephteach@hotmail.com | www.Peace-Together.com | www.ExploreLifeBlog.com

57

If you walk peaceful through your day,
you spread peace just by the act of
walking with awareness.

Joseph Bernard | Peace Together | Explore Life
josephteach@hotmail.com | www.Peace-Together.com | www.ExploreLifeBlog.com

58

Your emotions are often very energizing.
By turning towards them you will soon
move into more calming waters.

Joseph Bernard | Peace Together | Explore Life
josephteach@hotmail.com | www.Peace-Together.com | www.ExploreLifeBlog.com

59

Feel what you feel, let go of what needs to be released and then bask in peace.

Joseph Bernard | Peace Together | Explore Life
josephteach@hotmail.com | www.Peace-Together.com | www.ExploreLifeBlog.com

60

The busy mind is noisy, slow it down by being mindful and without judging. As judgment drops away so will the feelings of disharmony.

Joseph Bernard | Peace Together | Explore Life
josephteach@hotmail.com | www.Peace-Together.com | www.ExploreLifeBlog.com

61

Slow down and let your body come to
rest once in a while. Sit and feel the
peace of being present.

Joseph Bernard | Peace Together | Explore Life
josephteach@hotmail.com | www.Peace-Together.com | www.ExploreLifeBlog.com

62

Find peace today by shrinking your inner critic.
Instead have positive and supportive self-talk.

Joseph Bernard | Peace Together | Explore Life
josephteach@hotmail.com | www.Peace-Together.com | www.ExploreLifeBlog.com

63

Listen to your heart and love more freely.
Loving makes you feel most alive.

Joseph Bernard | Peace Together | Explore Life
josephteach@hotmail.com | www.Peace-Together.com | www.ExploreLifeBlog.com

64

Pay attention to your feelings. Make sure you are doing okay. They are always guiding you towards a more peaceful life.

Joseph Bernard | Peace Together | Explore Life
josephteach@hotmail.com | www.Peace-Together.com | www.ExploreLifeBlog.com

65

Spend time in the calmness of nature to feel
peace in the now of the natural world.

Joseph Bernard | Peace Together | Explore Life
josephteach@hotmail.com | www.Peace-Together.com | www.ExploreLifeBlog.com

66

Take a nap and dream about being peaceful
and enjoy the feelings when you wake up.

Joseph Bernard | Peace Together | Explore Life
josephteach@hotmail.com | www.Peace-Together.com | www.ExploreLifeBlog.com

67

Always pay close attention to your
intuition and act accordingly. You will
know peace in so many ways.

Joseph Bernard | Peace Together | Explore Life
josephteach@hotmail.com | www.Peace-Together.com | www.ExploreLifeBlog.com

68

Be more playful, do more fun things and laugh often. Let children show you the way.

Joseph Bernard | Peace Together | Explore Life
josephteach@hotmail.com | www.Peace-Together.com | www.ExploreLifeBlog.com

69

Express yourself creatively as a way to find joy,
aliveness, passion and peace.

Joseph Bernard | Peace Together | Explore Life
josephteach@hotmail.com | www.Peace-Together.com | www.ExploreLifeBlog.com

70

Thich Nhat Hahn is a great teacher of peace,
"breath in peace and breathe out a smile."

Joseph Bernard | Peace Together | Explore Life
josephteach@hotmail.com | www.Peace-Together.com | www.ExploreLifeBlog.com

71

Sing songs that uplift you. Listen to inspirational music and sense the body's harmonic response.

Joseph Bernard | Peace Together | Explore Life
josephteach@hotmail.com | www.Peace-Together.com | www.ExploreLifeBlog.com

72

Find where there are *Dances For Universal Peace* in your community and go join in the fun.

Joseph Bernard | Peace Together | Explore Life
josephteach@hotmail.com | www.Peace-Together.com | www.ExploreLifeBlog.com

73

Go for quiet and relaxing walks. Walking
meditation is even more peaceful.

Joseph Bernard | Peace Together | Explore Life
josephteach@hotmail.com | www.Peace-Together.com | www.ExploreLifeBlog.com

74

Listen to the birds sing, the sounds of a stream or the wind. In that appreciation of the now there will be peace.

Joseph Bernard | Peace Together | Explore Life
josephteach@hotmail.com | www.Peace-Together.com | www.ExploreLifeBlog.com

75

Feel gratitude for all you have
and for each moment.

Joseph Bernard | Peace Together | Explore Life
josephteach@hotmail.com | www.Peace-Together.com | www.ExploreLifeBlog.com

76

Expand your breathing and feel how alive
you are. Your breath is your life force
and a quiet way to find peace.

Joseph Bernard | Peace Together | Explore Life
josephteach@hotmail.com | www.Peace-Together.com | www.ExploreLifeBlog.com

77

See the beauty of the world around you,
there is a deep peace in the moments
of oneness with beauty.

Joseph Bernard | Peace Together | Explore Life
josephteach@hotmail.com | www.Peace-Together.com | www.ExploreLifeBlog.com

78

Finish unfinished stuff that is bothering you.
Leave the past where it belongs.

Joseph Bernard | Peace Together | Explore Life
josephteach@hotmail.com | www.Peace-Together.com | www.ExploreLifeBlog.com

79

Have friends that really listen. Be a
friend and listen too.

Joseph Bernard | *Peace Together* | *Explore Life*
josephteach@hotmail.com | *www.Peace-Together.com* | *www.ExploreLifeBlog.com*

80

Change beliefs that limit you and open
to more freedom in life.

Joseph Bernard | Peace Together | Explore Life
josephteach@hotmail.com | www.Peace-Together.com | www.ExploreLifeBlog.com

81

Say good riddance to guilt because it is not a real feeling, just one we learned from others.

Joseph Bernard | *Peace Together* | *Explore Life*
josephteach@hotmail.com | *www.Peace-Together.com* | *www.ExploreLifeBlog.com*

82

Stop watching the nightly news, you will
sleep much better and your mind will
be more at peace.

Joseph Bernard | Peace Together | Explore Life
josephteach@hotmail.com | www.Peace-Together.com | www.ExploreLifeBlog.com

83

Notice where fear runs you and change your thinking towards love. Love always trumps fear.

Joseph Bernard | Peace Together | Explore Life
josephteach@hotmail.com | www.Peace-Together.com | www.ExploreLifeBlog.com

84

Be kind to yourself. Love and
accept who you are.

Joseph Bernard | Peace Together | Explore Life
josephteach@hotmail.com | www.Peace-Together.com | www.ExploreLifeBlog.com

85

Do what feels right. Say no to what doesn't.

Joseph Bernard | Peace Together | Explore Life
josephteach@hotmail.com | www.Peace-Together.com | www.ExploreLifeBlog.com

86

Follow your own truth
and live by your values.

Joseph Bernard | Peace Together | Explore Life
josephteach@hotmail.com | www.Peace-Together.com | www.ExploreLifeBlog.com

87

Explore, express and enjoy your uniqueness
and share who you are with the world.

Joseph Bernard | Peace Together | Explore Life
josephteach@hotmail.com | www.Peace-Together.com | www.ExploreLifeBlog.com

88

Have a purpose in life and live it with passion.
Feel how good that feels.

Joseph Bernard | Peace Together | Explore Life
josephteach@hotmail.com | www.Peace-Together.com | www.ExploreLifeBlog.com

89

Only make commitments you can honor with
an open heart. Then follow through with
them in a peaceful manner.

Joseph Bernard | Peace Together | Explore Life
josephteach@hotmail.com | www.Peace-Together.com | www.ExploreLifeBlog.com

90

Focusing on the positive and expecting good things to happen will make life bring more peace to your mind and heart.

Joseph Bernard | Peace Together | Explore Life
josephteach@hotmail.com | www.Peace-Together.com | www.ExploreLifeBlog.com

91

Stop the noisy mind from blaming
and feel the peace that comes from taking
responsibility for your life.

Joseph Bernard | Peace Together | Explore Life
josephteach@hotmail.com | www.Peace-Together.com | www.ExploreLifeBlog.com

92

Explore where interests take you and be open
to the comfort of being on your own path.

Joseph Bernard | Peace Together | Explore Life
josephteach@hotmail.com | www.Peace-Together.com | www.ExploreLifeBlog.com

93

Wake up and see yourself having a wonderful day filled with joyous and peaceful moments.

Joseph Bernard | Peace Together | Explore Life
josephteach@hotmail.com | www.Peace-Together.com | www.ExploreLifeBlog.com

94

Find the peaceful place inside of you
and go visit there often.

Joseph Bernard | Peace Together | Explore Life
josephteach@hotmail.com | www.Peace-Together.com | www.ExploreLifeBlog.com

95

There is within you infinite possibilities.
Expressing those possibilities will change
you and the world around you.

Joseph Bernard | Peace Together | Explore Life
josephteach@hotmail.com | www.Peace-Together.com | www.ExploreLifeBlog.com

96

Take a step into the flow of life. Leave the worry
and hurry on the shore and float
peacefully in the moment.

Joseph Bernard | Peace Together | Explore Life
josephteach@hotmail.com | www.Peace-Together.com | www.ExploreLifeBlog.com

97

Mid-day, step away from what you are doing.
Move around and find yourself separate
from your doing and just be.

Joseph Bernard | Peace Together | Explore Life
josephteach@hotmail.com | www.Peace-Together.com | www.ExploreLifeBlog.com

98

Before you drift off to sleep remember what
you appreciate about you and your day,
then sleep in that appreciation.

Joseph Bernard | Peace Together | Explore Life
josephteach@hotmail.com | www.Peace-Together.com | www.ExploreLifeBlog.com

99

Find a place where you overlook your
community and sit in the peace
of where you live.

Joseph Bernard | Peace Together | Explore Life
josephteach@hotmail.com | www.Peace-Together.com | www.ExploreLifeBlog.com

100

Go to places that uplift you, take in the
vibrations, let yourself experience
the inspiration.

Joseph Bernard | Peace Together | Explore Life
josephteach@hotmail.com | www.Peace-Together.com | www.ExploreLifeBlog.com

101

An inactive body will make you restless. An active body will be more at peace.

Joseph Bernard | Peace Together | Explore Life
josephteach@hotmail.com | www.Peace-Together.com | www.ExploreLifeBlog.com

102

Allow your uniqueness to bloom into the most radiant expression of life.

Joseph Bernard | Peace Together | Explore Life
josephteach@hotmail.com | www.Peace-Together.com | www.ExploreLifeBlog.com

103

Tap into the stream of well-being and abundance, and enjoy the richness of life.

Joseph Bernard | *Peace Together* | *Explore Life*
josephteach@hotmail.com | *www.Peace-Together.com* | *www.ExploreLifeBlog.com*

104

Seek to balance the needs of your mind, body,
emotions and spirit. Nurturing each will
bring a contentment with life.

Joseph Bernard | Peace Together | Explore Life
josephteach@hotmail.com | www.Peace-Together.com | www.ExploreLifeBlog.com

PEACE
HEROES
TWEETS

There are peacemakers all around the world doing their best in shifting thoughts toward peace. They live ordinary lives but do extraordinary things — living their passion, exploring our inner worlds and spreading goodness and peace through their work. For this book, we've picked a few of those people that live an inspired life and are committed to sharing their wisdom so that we may all be inspired to reach for our dreams, find our passion, and become empowered to live to our fullest potential. For when we do that, we find a peace within our own lives that contributes to energy of the whole world, and our connections become brighter, more loving, and more peaceful.

About Bud Bilianich

I am a success coach, motivational speaker, author and blogger, and am well known for my common sense life and career success advice. I can help you create the successful life and career you want and deserve.

I was educated at Harvard, but have a no nonsense approach to my work that goes back to my roots in the steel country of Western Pennsylvania. My approach to life and career success is a result of over 35 years of business experience, 10 years of research and study of successful people and the application of common sense.

I am the author of 14 books, including the recently released *Success Tweets: 140 Bits of Common Sense Career Success Advice, All in 140 Characters or Less.* You can download a free copy of Success Tweets at *www.SuccessTweets.com.*

I have coached executives in some of the world's largest and best known companies. My client list reads like a Who's Who of the Fortune 500, and have been featured in *The Wall Street Journal, SUCCESS Magazine, Self Improvement Magazine* and a number of other success oriented publications.

You can contact me via my website at *www.BudBilanich.com,* or email, *Bud@BudBilanich.com.*

On Peace:

I believe that peace starts with me, and every other human being in this world. I do my best to live peace everyday by treating every person I meet with respect and dignity. I listen to what other people have to say, especially when I disagree with their point of view. I always look for, and usually find, common ground. I am content with who I am and what I have. I am happy when I see others succeed. I am there to support them when they fall short of their goals.

105

Peace is more than the absence of war or
hostility, it is being at harmony with yourself,
those close to you and the universe.

Bud Bilanich
The Common Sense Guy
Bud@BudBilanich.com | www.BudBilanich.com

106

Inner peace means being mentally and spiritually aligned with your circumstances. It's being strong in the face of discord or stress.

Bud Bilanich
The Common Sense Guy
Bud@BudBilanich.com | www.BudBilanich.com

107

Know and accept yourself to find inner peace.
Know and accept others to create
peace in this world.

Bud Bilanich
The Common Sense Guy
Bud@BudBilanich.com | www.BudBilanich.com

108

"Peace is not something you wish for.
It's something you make, something you do,
something you are, and something
you give away."

— Robert Fulghum

Bud Bilanich
The Common Sense Guy
Bud@BudBilanich.com | www.BudBilanich.com

109

Forgiveness precedes peace. Without forgiveness there can be no peace. Forgive others, more important, forgive yourself.

Bud Bilanich
The Common Sense Guy
Bud@BudBilanich.com | www.BudBilanich.com

110

When you're at peace with yourself and the world you're in a great place to build the successful life and career you want and deserve.

Bud Bilanich
The Common Sense Guy
Bud@BudBilanich.com | www.BudBilanich.com

111

War is not the way to peace. Benjamin Franklin was right — there was never a good war, nor a bad peace.

Bud Bilanich
The Common Sense Guy
Bud@BudBilanich.com | www.BudBilanich.com

112

"When the power of love overcomes the love of power, the world will know peace."

— Jimi Hendrix

Bud Bilanich
The Common Sense Guy
Bud@BudBilanich.com | www.BudBilanich.com

113

There is no blame, no resentments, no envy
and no payback on the road to peace.
Self acceptance and love of others are
around every corner.

Bud Bilanich
The Common Sense Guy
Bud@BudBilanich.com | www.BudBilanich.com

PEACE TWEETS

About Mary A. Casey, II

As the President of Boulder Quest Martial Arts and founder of Warrior Divas, my mission is to bring self defense and empowerment training to people in my communities, locally and worldwide. I coach people in getting out of the way of their success to live fully, freely, and fearlessly. To learn more, you can visit *boulderquest.com* or *warriordivas.com*.

As co-author of the blog "The Art of Winning: Eastern Strategies for Western Success", I write about how small shifts can make big changes. Whether it's theory, personal experience, or how-to information, the articles help you make a difference in your life. You can read my blog at *blog.boulderquest.com*.

What I believe:

- Life is too long for willpower. Instead, I cultivate a love of discipline, that internally-generated joy for doing things right and achieving my goals.
- To-Shin Do is ultimately about my Mind and Body agreeing on the best of course of action. When these are out of synch, I experience frustration, anger, and loss. When they harmonize, I am powerful, confident, and beautiful.
- When hardship first occurred I was a Victim, then I was a Survivor. Now I am a Warrior.

On being a warrior for peace:

Non-violence isn't peace nor is it passivity. Peace is engaging the world with your purest heart and noblest ideals. It is so important for every person to have an active practice in a safe environment that allows them to test their centeredness. I have learned that I can never know enough but the journey is worth every step.

114

If you are afraid of the consequences, you cannot be at peace in your heart.

Mary A. Casey II
Boulder Quest Center & Warrior Devas
aitoshi@BoulderQuest.com | www.BoulderQuest.com | www.WarriorDevas.com

PEACE TWEETS

115

Complacency is the enemy of peace.

Mary A. Casey II
Boulder Quest Center & Warrior Devas
aitoshi@BoulderQuest.com | www.BoulderQuest.com | www.WarriorDevas.com

126

116

Dare to exceed your potential.

Mary A. Casey II
Boulder Quest Center & Warrior Devas
aitoshi@BoulderQuest.com | *www.BoulderQuest.com* | *www.WarriorDevas.com*

117

A warrior appreciates the defeats
as well as the victories.

Mary A. Casey II
Boulder Quest Center & Warrior Devas
aitoshi@BoulderQuest.com | www.BoulderQuest.com | www.WarriorDevas.com

PEACE TWEETS

118

A peaceful warrior celebrates
the joy of discipline.

Mary A. Casey II
Boulder Quest Center & Warrior Devas
aitoshi@BoulderQuest.com | www.BoulderQuest.com | www.WarriorDevas.com

129

119

Peace is magical.

Mary A. Casey II
Boulder Quest Center & Warrior Devas
aitoshi@BoulderQuest.com | *www.BoulderQuest.com* | *www.WarriorDevas.com*

120

Peaceful thoughts without supporting
action only effects yourself.

Mary A. Casey II
Boulder Quest Center & Warrior Devas
aitoshi@BoulderQuest.com | www.BoulderQuest.com | www.WarriorDevas.com

121

Your intention + Your actions = Your results.

Mary A. Casey II
Boulder Quest Center & Warrior Devas
aitoshi@BoulderQuest.com | www.BoulderQuest.com | www.WarriorDevas.com

122

The warrior takes on all challenges with a clear heart, open mind, and willing self.

Mary A. Casey II
Boulder Quest Center & Warrior Devas
aitoshi@BoulderQuest.com | www.BoulderQuest.com | www.WarriorDevas.com

PEACE TWEETS

About Chris Guillebeau

My mission is to help people live unconventional lives, make their own choices, and change the world. As I define it, nonconformity is not merely about opposing something; the idea is to stand for something. It's too easy to be a cynic. It's better to be a believer.

The Art of Non-Conformity (AONC) project chronicles my writing on how to change the world by achieving significant, personal goals while helping others at the same time. In the battle against conventional beliefs, we focus on three areas: Life, Work, and Travel.

Twice a week I write on at least one of those topics, and once in a while I profile other revolutionaries who are also changing the world through unconventional ways. You can find my blog at *chrisguillebeau.com*.

More specifically:

- I write about personal development and life planning, with the conviction that you don't have to live your life the way other people expect you to.
- I write about entrepreneurship and other kinds of unconventional work, with the belief that the work we do should be both fun and meaningful.
- I write about international travel, travel hacking in general, and my journeys to more than 25 countries every year.

On Peace:

My worldview about peace comes from the time I spent in post-war Africa. Unfortunately, I learned that it's much easier to destroy than to create. But fortunately, I learned that the process of rebuilding is inspiring and intensely meaningful.

123

There is almost always more than one way
to accomplish something.

Chris Guillebeau | *Art of Non-Conformity Site: http://ChrisGuillebeau.com*
140-character version: @chrisguillebeau | *chris.guillebeau@gmail.com*

124

You don't have to live your life the way
other people expect you to.

Chris Guillebeau | *Art of Non-Conformity Site: http://ChrisGuillebeau.com*
140-character version: @chrisguillebeau | *chris.guillebeau@gmail.com*

125

You can do good things for yourself and help other people at the same time.

Chris Guillebeau | *Art of Non-Conformity Site: http://ChrisGuillebeau.com*
140-character version: @chrisguillebeau | *chris.guillebeau@gmail.com*

126

If you don't decide for yourself what you want
to get out of life, someone else will probably
end up deciding for you.

Chris Guillebeau | *Art of Non-Conformity Site: http://ChrisGuillebeau.com*
140-character version: @chrisguillebeau | chris.guillebeau@gmail.com

127

Once you fully understand what you want,
it's not usually that difficult to get it.

Chris Guillebeau | *Art of Non-Conformity Site: http://ChrisGuillebeau.com*
140-character version: @chrisguillebeau | *chris.guillebeau@gmail.com*

128

Many of us live our lives out of the fear of
what other people think of us. We're waiting
for someone to give us permission to
be ourselves.

Chris Guillebeau | Art of Non-Conformity Site: http://ChrisGuillebeau.com
140-character version: @chrisguillebeau | chris.guillebeau@gmail.com

129

Don't try to be fearless or pretend you aren't impacted by fear. Just try to prevent fear from making your decisions for you.

Chris Guillebeau | Art of Non-Conformity Site: http://ChrisGuillebeau.com
140-character version: @chrisguillebeau | chris.guillebeau@gmail.com

130

Embracing reality may be exhausting, but I can't imagine the alternative of avoiding it.

Chris Guillebeau | Art of Non-Conformity Site: http://ChrisGuillebeau.com
140-character version: @chrisguillebeau | chris.guillebeau@gmail.com

131

Hope defeats fear, and abundance defeats scarcity. Which side do you want to be on?

Chris Guillebeau | *Art of Non-Conformity Site: http://ChrisGuillebeau.com*
140-character version: @chrisguillebeau | *chris.guillebeau@gmail.com*

About Ani Bell

I'm a risk-takin', rainmakin', rule breakin' life coach | writer | speaker. I've lost and found my way on the Blissful-Life-Path more times than I can count.

After 45 years of trekking and climbing and laughing and crying and stumbling and rolling and learning and growing — I decided to stop following — *and start leading.*

What if I lead with my heart, NO MATTER WHAT? No matter the money, the skeptics, the fear — or the consequences.

What happens if I do what I want, when I want, as much or as little as I want — in every aspect of life and work?

What if I do only what feels good?

On March 6, 2010, I began a *RADICAL SABBATICAL* experiment, taking a break from the *have to's* and *should's* and from believing in 'it can't be done' and 'impossible' — and decided to answer these tantalizing questions for myself, one day at a time.

So far, so good! I've discovered a place of deep peace within — and am sharing my experiences with the masses via sporadic-spunky-insanely-honest (and free!) *RADICAL SABBATICAL* eblast updates.

On Peace:

I have an unshakeable faith that all of us can achieve individual inner peace, and — once enough of us do so — the magnificent energy that results will empower us to create Heaven-On-Earth. *YES!*

132

Let go of resisting *what is.* Reach for a better thought. Harness that good-thought-energy and allow *what isn't* to reveal itself.

Ani Bell | Free Spirit! | ani@anibell.com | 406.222.7421

133

Gently and powerfully tell the truth about what you deeply, authentically want. To yourself. In the mirror. *Now.*

Ani Bell | Free Spirit! | ani@anibell.com | 406.222.7421

134

You get what you expect. So expect the best!
Expect that things go well for you. They will.
Expect to live a charmed life. You will.

Ani Bell | Free Spirit! | ani@anibell.com | 406.222.7421

135

Be willing to be wrong, to be late, to miss the deadline. It's not the end of the world. *Really.*

Ani Bell | Free Spirit! | ani@anibell.com | 406.222.7421

136

What is going 'right' in your life? Focus thought-energy there, and soon more things will begin to go 'right'.

Ani Bell | Free Spirit! | ani@anibell.com | 406.222.7421

137

You don't have to 'get in the flow'. The truth is you are already in it. You only need allow it in. Allow. Allow. Allow.

Ani Bell | Free Spirit! | ani@anibell.com | 406.222.7421

138

Deeply care about how you feel and make feeling good your number one priority. *Your number one priority.* No if's, and's or but's.

Ani Bell | Free Spirit! | ani@anibell.com | 406.222.7421

139

Care not about what others think, say or do about what you are thinking, saying or doing.

Ani Bell | Free Spirit! | ani@anibell.com | 406.222.7421

140

Rest easy. The weight of the world is not on your shoulders. It's on *our* shoulders. Together — *we can do this.*

Ani Bell | Free Spirit! | ani@anibell.com | 406.222.7421

www.ingramcontent.com/pod-product-compliance
Lightning Source LLC
Chambersburg PA
CBHW072126280526
45788CB00002B/569